PowerKids Readers:

EARTH MOVERS™

Dump Trucks

Joanne Randolph

The Rosen Publishing Group's
PowerKids Press™
New York

1

For Ryan, with love

Published in 2002 by The Rosen Publishing Group, Inc.
29 East 21st Street, New York, NY 10010

First Edition

Book Design: Michael Donnellan

Photo Credits: pp. 5, 9, 11, 13, and 17 © Highway Images/Bette S. Garber; pp. 7, 15, 19, and 21 © SuperStock.

Randolph, Joanne.
Dump trucks / Joanne Randolph.
    p. cm. — (Earth movers)
Includes bibliographical references and index.
ISBN 0-8239-6027-7 (library binding)
1. Dump trucks—Juvenile literature. [1. Dump trucks.] I. Title.
TL230.15 .R35 2002
629.225—dc21

                                            2001000146

Manufactured in the United States of America

2

Contents

This is a dump truck.

Dump trucks carry dirt and rocks. They dump the dirt and rocks into piles.

Look at the dirt in this dump truck. The dirt is called the load.

The dump truck carries the load in the back. The back part is sometimes called a bed.

49

The back of the dump truck tips. This makes it easy to dump out the load.

13

This dump truck was filled with dirt. It tilted until the load fell out. Then there was a big pile of dirt.

15

Other trucks help fill the dump truck with dirt.

Sometimes there is a lot of dirt to be taken away. Many dump trucks are needed. There are three dump trucks here.

Dump trucks are very busy machines.

21

Words to Know

bed

dump truck

load

Here are more books to read about dump trucks:

Diggers and Dump Trucks
(Eye Openers)
By Angela Royston
Little Simon

Truck: and other building machines
(Mighty Machines)
By Claire Llewellyn
Dorling Kindersley

To learn more about dump trucks, check out these Web sites:
www.howstuffworks.com/hydraulic7.htm
www.komatsu.co.jp/kikki/zukan/e_index.htm

23

Index

Word Count: 125
Note to Librarians, Teachers, and Parents

PowerKids Readers are specially designed to help emergent and beginning readers build their skills in reading for information. Simple vocabulary and concepts are paired with photographs of real kids in real-life situations or stunning, detailed images from the natural world around them. Readers will respond to written language by linking meaning with their own everyday experiences and observations. Sentences are short and simple, employing a basic vocabulary of sight words, as well as new words that describe objects or processes that take place in the natural world. Large type, clean design, and photographs corresponding directly to the text all help children to decipher meaning. Features such as a contents page, picture glossary, and index help children get the most out of PowerKids Readers. They also introduce children to the basic elements of a book, which they will encounter in their future reading experiences. Lists of related books and Web sites encourage kids to explore other sources and to continue the process of learning.

24